Editorial Project Manager
Mara Ellen Guckian

Illustrator
Kelly McMahon

Cover Artist
Courtney Barnes

Editor in Chief
Ina Massler Levin, M.A.

Creative Director
Karen J. Goldfluss, M.S. Ed.

Art Production Manager
Kevin Barnes

Art Coordinator
Renée Christine Yates

Imaging
James Edward Grace

Publisher

Mary D. Smith, M.S. Ed.

S0-ATS-388

Pre·K to 2nd

Author

Katrina Cavaliere

Teacher Created Resources, Inc.
6421 Industry Way
Westminster, CA 92683
www.teachercreated.com

ISBN: 978-1-4206-2002-3

© 2008 Teacher Created Resources, Inc.
Reprinted, 2011
Made in U.S.A.

Teacher Created Resources

Table of Contents

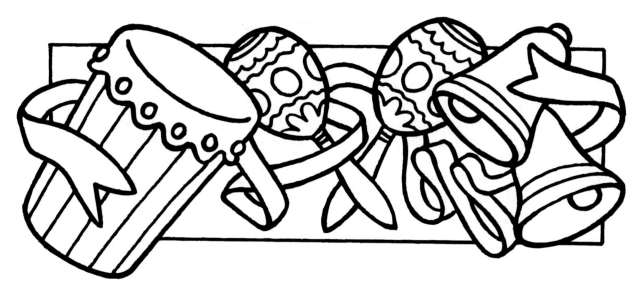

Introduction

Why teach music to your students? Singing and playing instruments are wonderful, constructive ways to channel children's energy. If you expose children to music at a young age, there is a greater chance that their appreciation of it will continue as they mature, broadening possibilities for their future. Music can make an incredible difference in a child's life.

Several studies have shown that preschoolers' spatial reasoning scores increase dramatically when they are given musical training in group singing classes and piano classes. Many of the songs contained in this book reinforce students' undertanding of spatial concepts, directionality, opposites, rhyme, and vocabulary. Kids involved in music also tend to receive higher test scores and receive higher grades in school. Participation in music helps develop self-esteem and collaborative skills.

Students can learn to appreciate music in many ways. Not every child has a great voice, but all children can improve their singing voices with practice. Also, keep in mind, there is more to music than singing. Use dancing, marching, and movement to generate enthusiasm. This book contains songs, movement, and directions for crafting musical instruments. Allowing students to move about when singing songs or playing instruments will lend to the excitement. Let them feel the beat with their feet while marching and/or playing instruments. Students can dance waving scarves, streamers, flags or little blankets. Invite students to put on mini-performances and share their enthusiasm with others.

Put on some classical music with different tempos (speeds) and different dynamics (volume). Encourage young musicians to express the differences they hear with their movements. Try dancing and swinging scarves to fast music and then switching to a slower tempo. Note the different movements the scarves make and describe these motions. Try suggesting big movements for loud music and smaller movements for quieter music. Discuss these differences with students as well.

Classical pieces of music are good for demonstrating these opposites. Stravinsky's *Firebird* is one such piece. *The Sorcerer's Apprentice* by Dukas is another great piece of dance music. Many children's movies have great soundtracks you can move to in the classroom. Jazz, classical, reggae, and rock can be used to get your students excited about music.

You can help foster your children's interest in music at a very young age. The melodies of the songs in this book are traditional ones. They are easy to sing and use at home and in the classroom. You don't have to be a great singer to have fun singing together. Just start singing!

Getting Started

Introduce students to percussion instruments. All percussion instruments create sound by being hit, scraped or shaken. Drums, cymbals, shakers, and xylophones are all percussion instruments. Many percussion instruments have drum heads—a material stretched tightly across the frame of the drum. Then the drum head is struck by a stick, mallet, or even hands. Even the piano is considered a percussion instrument. When the keys of a piano are pushed down, a string is hit on the inside of the piano with something called a hammer. Xylophones, bells and marimbas are keyboard instruments. They look like piano keyboards but are played with mallets.

To enhance the students' understanding of the sounds that percussion instruments make, play music in which you can hear those instruments. Shakers and other percussion instruments can be heard in jazz, calypso, and classical music. You can hear these instruments being played on many children's music CDs. Most percussion instruments are used to supply a beat for a band. Once you have discussed percussion instruments and shared pictures of them, introduce the worksheet on page 5.

Percussion instruments are easy and inexpensive to make and even easier to play! The following pages provide directions for making a variety of percussion instruments including drums, different types of shakers, and sticks. While making the musical instruments described in this book, play music in which the instruments you are simulating can be heard. Later, each type of instrument can be introduced with the featured song. Words to additonal songs are provided in subsequent sections. These songs can be accompanied by one or more of the instruments created. Most songs lend themselves to any of the instruments constructed. The songs in this book are arranged in sections:

- **Musical Instruments and Songs**
  The musical crafts use basic materials and are easy to create. Your musicians will be playing them in no time with the suggested songs.

- **Counting Songs**
  Sing, move, and use drum sticks with these fun songs that reinforce counting forward and backwards. Many believe that music and math are linked together. What do you think?

- **Transitional Songs**
  From group time to cleaning up, there are songs to be sung while starting a new activity. These songs are short and easy to remember but get the job done!

- **Everyday Songs**
  Music has a way of engaging students, lightening a mood and building cooperative skills. Once students are familiar with these songs, try adding instruments.

- **Songs for Dancing and Movement**
  Get those kids movin'! Dancing and movement songs are meant to keep children active while singing. These songs are good songs to use when kids are high on energy and low on sitting still.

- **Student Input Songs**
  Children love it when they have a say in something. Allow them to be creative by choosing things to sing about within a song. It might be choosing which animal to sing about on Old McDonald's farm, or what sounds animals will make.

- **Songs for Seasons and Holidays**
  What school year is complete without discussing seasons and holidays? These songs can be accompanied by instruments but do not require them. Each holiday song is on its own page. Students can decorate the pages and create a holiday book or use them to decorate the classroom.

- **Performance Song**
  A longer song can work well for school performances and special events. Teach this type of song after your musicians are comfortable singing together. Incorporate movements and dance with playing their musical instruments. Props can be included to further enhance the presentation.

Percussion Instruments

Directions: Color the 10 percussion instruments below and circle your favorite.

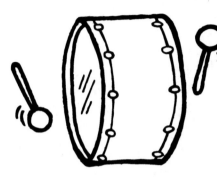

bass drum

bells

cymbals

maracas

marimba

snare drum

tambourine

timpani

triangle

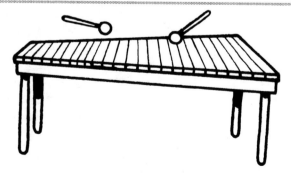

xylophone

Drums

Before making drums, discuss with students what they know about drums. Ask if they have ever seen or heard a drum before. Do they have some type of drum at home? Have they seen drums at parades, concerts, or at football games?

Explain that drums are percussion instruments and that there are many different kinds of drums. Share pictures or examples, if possible. Practice playing drums by tapping tables, desks, or the floor. Discuss different ways to play a drum using one's hands—*loud*, *soft*, *fast*, *slow*, etc. Focus on the different sounds as students use different surfaces to play.

Drum Materials

- empty, cylindrical oatmeal containers
- construction paper or craft paper
- markers, crayons or colored pencils
- tape

Optional Materials

- stickers
- contact paper (select a colorful pattern or solid color)
- clear contact paper or laminate

Making a Drum

1. Cut the construction paper long enough to wrap it around the oatmeal container and have a 1-inch overlap (illustration). Cut an additional circle to fit on the lid or use stickers.
2. Use markers or crayons to decorate and/or personalize the construction paper. Laminate, if possible, for durability.
3. Tape the paper to the container.

Teacher Note: You may not want students to personalize the drums if they are being made to be used by various groups of musicians. Colored or patterned contact paper works well if you are planning on using the drums with multiple classrooms or if you plan on using them long term.

Drums *(cont.)*

Practice playing the new drums. Have the students place their drums on a table or on the floor. Tap the drum head loudly and get progressively softer. Try tapping quickly and then change to a slower tempo, etc. Later, when students are comfortable, have them stand and hold the drum using one arm while they play with the other hand.

Another enjoyable activity is to use the drums to simulate the sounds of a storm. Start by lightly tapping fingers on the drum. Begin tapping harder and harder and suggest that the storm is getting stronger. Beat the drums for a while and then slowly begin to tap more gently. Try to go very slowly "until the storm stops."

Talk with students about marching. When you *march* you move your feet to the beat of the music. Have they ever seen a marching band in a parade or at a sporting event? Marching is a way of *feeling* music. When students learn to march in time to the music (especially if they are also singing or playing a drum or shaker), they are connecting their aural world with their physical world. These types of connections help students to use both sides of their brain simultaneously.

Practice marching around the classroom in single file. Choose different students to be the leader as you march. Try marching in a circle or other shape. Pair the students up and have them march around in twos. Once students are familiar with marching, you can apply this technique to any song to help them feel the music and release a little energy as well.

Hit Your Drum

(Sing to the tune of "London Bridge.")

Hit your drum now really hard,
Really hard,
Really hard.
Hit your drum now really hard,
Make it loud!

Hit your drum now really soft,
Really soft,
Really soft.
Hit your drum now really soft,
Play it softly.

Shakers

Shakers are hand-held percussion instruments. They are hollow containers that can be filled with a variety of materials and sealed. Some have handles such as maracas, but a simple film canister filled with rice also makes a great shaker. If possible, share different types of shakers with students. Allow students time to try them out and compare them.

- When you shake the shakers, what do they sound like?
- Can you shake them slowly, quickly, softly, and loudly (opposites)?
- Does what is inside the container affect the sound?
- Does the amount in the container affect the sound?

There are three types of shaker crafts suggested in this book. All of them use recyclable materials and are simple to make and decorate. By adding different materials (rice, beans, gravel, unpopped popcorn, etc.) and varying quantities in the containers, the shakers will make a variety of sounds. The following shaker song can be used with any of the shaker instruments listed in this book.

Shake It

(Sing to the tune of "Mary Had a Little Lamb.")

Shake your shaker over your head,
Over your head, over your head.
Shake your shaker over your head, let's start shaking.

Shake your shaker near the ground,
Near the ground, near the ground.
Shake your shaker near the ground, keep on shaking.

Shake it really loud and fast,
Loud and fast, loud and fast,
Shake it really loud and fast, keep on shaking.

Shake it really soft and slow,
Soft and slow, soft and slow.
Shake it really soft and slow, keep on shaking.

Shake your shaker any way,
Any way, any way,
Shake your shaker any way, now stop shaking.

8

Shakers *(cont.)*

Plate Shakers

Materials

- 2 paper plates (or plastic for louder, sturdier shakers) per shaker
- unpopped popcorn, dried beans, or rice
- 4-inch strips of crate or crepe paper, streamers, or ribbons
- stickers and other materials to decorate
- crayons or markers
- glue
- *optional:* stapler or glue gun

Safety Note: Adult supervision will be required if using a glue gun. Glue guns work best when using plastic plates instead of paper.

Making a Plate Shaker

1. Decorate the bottoms of the plates with stickers, crayons, markers, yarn, etc. and let them dry.
2. Lay one plate flat on a table and make a line of glue around the edge. Place the 4-inch strips of paper on the glue, around the edge of the plate.
3. Carefully fill that plate (about 1/2 full) with dried beans, beads, or unpopped popcorn.
4. Add more glue on top of the paper strips.
5. Press the second plate on top of the first plate.

Note: A stapler or glue gun may be used for a stronger hold.

Plate Decorating Ideas

Pumpkins—Paint the plates orange or use orange plates. Cut out shapes to create pumpkin faces (patterns provided on page 10).

Turkeys—Paint the plates brown or use brown plates. Cut out feather shapes to make a tail. Add eyes, a beak, a wattle, and feet or use the turkey head pattern provided (page 11).

Snowmen—Use white plates. Cut out shapes to make faces using the patterns provided on page 11, or draw them using crayons or markers.

Sun—Paint the plates yellow or use yellow plates. Add cut-out shapes to create a face for the sun. Add yellow strips for rays.

Picture Frame Plates—Have each child bring in a picture of himself or herself or the family, a pet, etc. Color the plate and then glue the pictures in the middle of the plates.

Personalized Plates—Allow students to paint and decorate as they choose.

Plate Shaker Patterns

Pumpkin Faces

Plate Shaker Patterns *(cont.)*

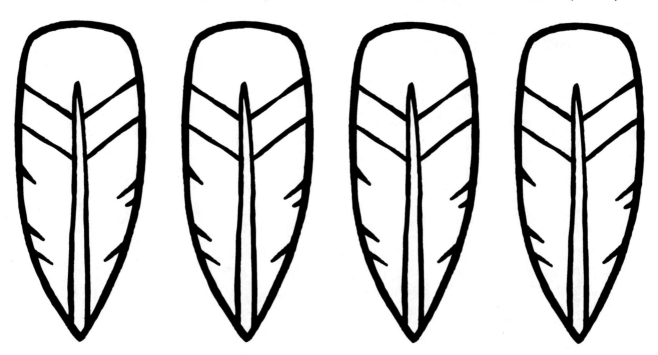

Turkey Feathers

Snowman Face   **Turkey Head**

Shakers *(cont.)*

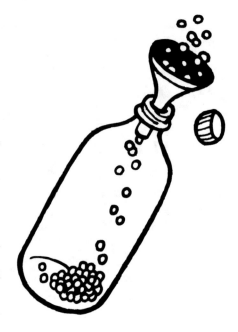

Plastic Bottle Shakers

Materials

- clean, empty plastic carbonated drink bottles (with caps)
- unpopped popcorn, beans, or small, colorful fish tank rocks
- yarn
- stickers
- funnels

Making Plastic Bottle Shaker

1. Fill the plastic bottle about 1/4 full with one of the materials listed above to create sounds. Consider giving different sound materials to different groups of students.

2. Decorate the bottle by gluing on ribbon or yarn, or by using stickers.

What Is in the Bottle

(Sing to the tune of "Row, Row, Row Your Boat.")

What is in the bottle?
Shake it and you'll hear.
Shake it high, shake it low,
Shake it high, shake it low,
Let's all give a cheer!

Shakers *(cont.)*

"Hot Cross Bun" Can Shakers

Materials

- clean, empty drink cans
- unpopped popcorn, rice, beans or other material
- brown construction paper
- white crayons or tape
- scissors
- electrician's tape
- glue

Making a Can Shaker

1. Fill the drink can about 1/4 full with popcorn kernels, rice, beans or other material.
2. Place tape over the opening at the top of the can.
3. Cut brown construction paper to wrap around the can (your bun).
4. Tape or glue the brown paper into place.
5. Use a white crayon to draw criss-cross lines for frosting on the "buns."

Hot Cross Buns

(Traditional)

Hot cross buns!
Hot cross buns!
One a penny,
Two a penny,
Hot cross buns!

Shakers *(cont.)*

Egg Shakers

Materials

- plastic eggs (that can be opened)
- unpopped popcorn, beans or rice
- stickers or colored masking tape

Teacher Note: Colorful plastic eggs are available in many stores and craft shops in the spring. Stock up if you see them!

Making Egg Shakers

1. Separate the plastic eggs. You may wish to have a pile of tops and another pile of bottoms. Allow students choose one half egg from each pile. When combined, they will be more colorful.

2. Pour unpopped popcorn, dried beans or rice into one egg half.

3. Carefully put the egg halves together.

4. Place stickers or tape over the egg seam to hold the halves together.

Presentation

Start with the lines below sung to the tune of "Row, Row, Row Your Boat." This rhyme will also allow practice with directional words *left* and *right*. For additional practice use a made-up melody or speak the words, rap style, using the poem on page 15. Each line will guide students toward the preferred shaker movement. This activity gives students opportunities to demonstrate vocabulary knowledge and practice both opposites and spatial concepts. Encourage your musicians to contribute a rhyme or two as they become more familiar with the Shake Your Eggs song. The refrain is also a great way to practice left and right directions.

Shake Your Egg

(Sing to the tune of "Row, Row, Row Your Boat.")

Shake, shake, shake your egg.

Shake it left then right!

Trade your shaker with a friend,

Shake it with all your might!

Shakers *(cont.)*

Shake Your Eggs

Shake your eggs up real high,
(Shake eggs over your head.)

Shake them low, oh me oh my!
(Shake the eggs toward the ground.)

Shake them left and shake them right,
(Shake them to your left and then to your right.)

Shake the eggs with all your might!
(Shake the eggs vigorously in front of you.)

Shake them slowly, all around,
(Shake the eggs slowly in a circular motion.)

Shake them quickly, hear the sound!
(Shake the eggs quickly.)

Shake them left and shake them right,
(Shake them to your left and then to your right.)

Shake your eggs with all your might!
(Shake the eggs vigorously in front of you.)

Sticks

Materials

- two 12" dowels per musician
- markers or colored tape

A note about dowels: Dowels come in a variety of widths. You may wish to have all the dowels be the same size, or you may wish to have a variety of different widths to produce different sounds. They can be purchased and cut (for a fee) in most large hardware stores. Dowels are also found in many large craft stores (some are sold pre-cut in packages of 6 or more).

Making Sticks

1. Give each student two sticks to personalize.
2. Use markers to color the sticks or attach pieces of colored tape.
3. Add initials on the bottom of each pair of sticks if they are to be kept by the student. If not, store the sticks together in a large container and allow musicians to choose two each time.

Presentation

Before using the sticks to play music, have a safety discussion. Remind your musicians that the sticks are serving as musical instruments. Caution against poking or waving them around or near another musician's face or body.

Practice hitting the sticks on the floor by alternating the sticks (right hand then left hand) or by hitting the floor simultaneously. Practice hitting the sticks together. Then practice alternating hitting the sticks on the floor and then together. After your musicians are comfortable playing their sticks in these ways, apply these techniques while singing the ABC song.

ABC's
(Traditional)

A B C D E F G
H I J K
L M N O P
Q R S
T U V
W
X
Y and Z
Now I know my ABC's.
Next time won't you sing with me?

Sticks *(cont.)*

Jingle Bell Sticks

Materials

- large jingle bells
- leather laces (can be bought on spools at craft stores)
- plastic (not wooden) paint stir sticks with holes from hardware store
- colored felt
- *optional:* stickers

Making Jingle Bell Sticks

1. Cut the felt long enough to wrap around the paint stick (the stirrer end, not the handle).
2. Glue the felt to the stirrer end of the stick.
3. Create holes in the felt with scissors where the holes in the paint sticks are located.

   Safety Note: Adult assistance is advised for this step.
4. Cut the leather laces long enough to thread through the holes and tie on the back side of the sticks.
5. Thread the jingle bells onto the leather laces.
6. Thread the leather laces through the holes in the felt-covered sticks.
7. Tie the laces in knots to secure the jingle bells.
8. Add stickers to the instruments for decoration.

Sticks (cont.)

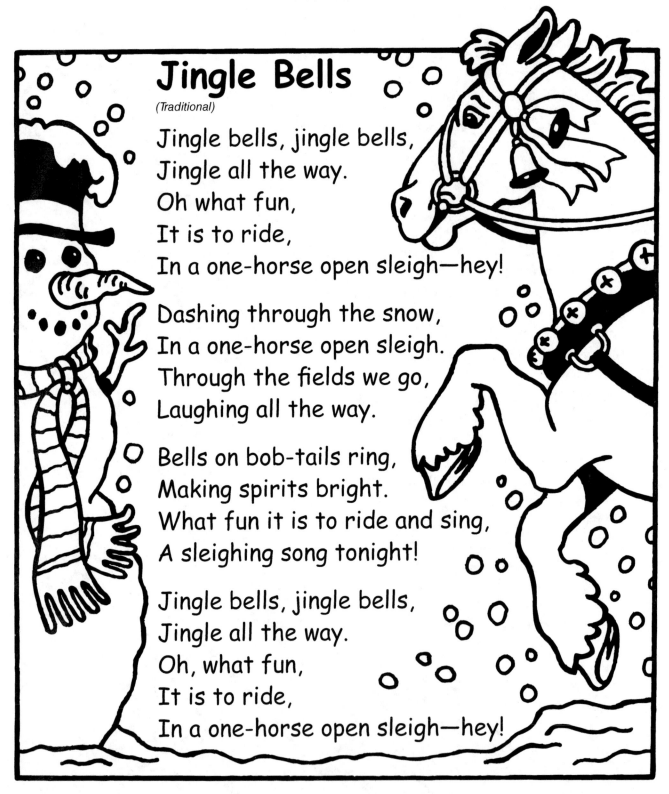

Jingle Bells

(Traditional)

Jingle bells, jingle bells,
Jingle all the way.
Oh what fun,
It is to ride,
In a one-horse open sleigh—hey!

Dashing through the snow,
In a one-horse open sleigh.
Through the fields we go,
Laughing all the way.

Bells on bob-tails ring,
Making spirits bright.
What fun it is to ride and sing,
A sleighing song tonight!

Jingle bells, jingle bells,
Jingle all the way.
Oh, what fun,
It is to ride,
In a one-horse open sleigh—hey!

Suggestion: Another song to use with the jingle bell sticks year round is "*Shake Your Eggs*" (page 15). While singing the song, replace the word "eggs" with "bells." For example: "Shake your eggs up real high" now becomes... "Shake your bells up real high."

Counting Songs

Teach your musicians counting songs and then add the movements with the dowel drumsticks. What better way to introduce counting forward and backward than with a song! Your musicians will be doing math in their heads before they know it.

Five Little Monkeys Swinging in the Tree

(Traditional)

Five little monkeys
    swinging in the tree,
(Swing sticks back and forth.)

Teasing Mr. Alligator,
    You can't catch me,
(Wiggle the sticks as if you are teasing the alligator.)

Along comes Mr. Alligator
    quiet as can be,
(Put sticks together and act as if they are moving like a swimming alligator.)

And snaps that monkey
    right out of that tree!
(Hit the sticks together.)

Additional Verses
    Four little monkeys. . .
    Three little monkeys. . .
    Two little monkeys. . .
    One little monkey. . .

Suggested Instrument: Dowel Sticks

One, Two, Buckle My Shoe

(Traditional)

One, two, buckle my shoe.
(Pretend to tie a shoe.)

Three, four, close the door.
(Hit sticks together.)

Five, six, pick up sticks.
(Set down the sticks and pick them up.)

Seven, eight, lay them straight.
(Lay down sticks.)

Nine, ten, this is the end!
(Leave the sticks on the floor and hold up empty hands.)

Alternate Ending: Say, "Nine, ten, let's do it again!" and then sing the entire song over again as many times as you want. End with "Nine, ten, this is the end!"

Suggestion: Teach your musicians the counting songs and then keep time with the dowel sticks.

One Little, Two Little, Three Little...

(Sing to the tune of "One Little, Two Little, Three Little Indians.")

One little, two little, three little pumpkins
Four little, five little, six little pumpkins
Seven little, eight little, nine little pumpkins
Ten little pumpkins glowing bright.

Variations

This song works well when studying a specific unit at school. It also lends itself well to seasons and holidays. At Halloween they might suggest counting pumpkins, ghosts or owls. During the winter, the children might choose to count/sing about snowflakes or snowballs.

For example:

One little, two little, three little owls
Four little, five little, six little owls
Seven little, eight little, nine little owls
Ten little owls, hooting all night.

Or,

One little, two little, three little snowflakes
Four little, five little, six little snowflakes
Seven little, eight little, nine little snowflakes
Ten little snowflakes falling on the ground.

Song Considerations

Before starting the song, agree upon the last few words in the last verse. An alternate ending for the first example below might be: Ten little pumpkins rolling on the ground. Or... ten little pumpkins, big and round.

If you are talking about a specific letter of the alphabet, suggestions for that day might have to be things that start with that letter.

Another way to end the song is to have the teacher be the only one to sing the end of the song. This will save time and the children won't need to remember the last line when you get to it. Have all the children sing the whole song until the words following "ten little pumpkins."

If you have a talent for being creative with words, you might make your children laugh with your ending. For example, if you are counting monsters you might end with "ten little monsters chasing you" and reach out to tickle the children. Or end the same verse with "ten little monsters all shouting BOO!" and get the children saying boo to one another—it can be very contagious!

This Old Man

(Traditional)

This old man, he played **one,**
He played knick knack on his thumb.
(Tap thumb with stick one time.)

Refrain

With a knick knack paddy whack
Give the dog a bone,
This old man came rolling home.

This old man, he played **two,**
He played knick knack on his shoes.
(Tap shoes with sticks two times.)

Refrain

With a knick knack paddy whack
Give the dog a bone,
This old man came rolling home.

This old man, he played **three,**
He played knick knack on his knee.
(Tap knees with sticks three times.)

Refrain

With a knick knack paddy whack
Give the dog a bone,
This old man came rolling home.

This old man, he played **four,**
He played knick knack on the floor.
(Hit the floor gently with sticks four times.)

Refrain

With a knick knack paddy whack
Give the dog a bone,
This old man came rolling home.

This old man, he played **five,**
He played knick knack on beehives.
(Hit sticks together loudly five times.)

Refrain

With a knick knack paddy whack
Give the dog a bone,
This old man came rolling home.

The Ants Go Marching

Singing "The Ants Go Marching" is a great way to introduce or reinforce rhyming words, marching, and counting down from 10 to one.

To start, have students sit in a circle with their drums on the floor in front of them. Practice singing the first verse of the song. When you sing the words "the little one stops to..." Show them the motion for that verse (i.e. - pretend to suck their thumbs). Once the children have an understanding of the motions for each verse, have them stand in a circle and hold their drums in one hand. Explain that they will beat the drum with the other hand while marching.

The next step is to get the children following one another around the circle. Once they are moving, start the song. When you sing "the little one stops to..." have them set their drums on the floor and do the motions. Once you have done the motion for that verse, pick up the drums and sing, "and they all go marching down..." and start marching around the circle once again.

Variations

1. To add variety, change the words at the end of each verse. Children can even help create this song by coming up with rhyming words to use.

2. Another phrase that can be added to any number (especially good with numbers that are hard to find rhymes with—like seven) is the little one stopped and counted to 1, 2, 3 or whatever number you are on. For example, the little one stopped to count up to seven (then instead of doing a motion like climbing a tree, take a few seconds to count out loud 1, 2, 3, 4, 5, 6, 7).

The Ants Go Marching (cont.)

(Traditional)

The ants go marching one by one, hurrah, hurrah!
The ants go marching one by one, hurrah, hurrah!
The ants go marching one by one,
The little one stops to suck his thumb,
And they all go marching down to the ground
To get out of the rain, **boom, boom, boom!**

The ants go marching two by two, hurrah, hurrah!
The ants go marching two by two, hurrah, hurrah!
The ants go marching two by two,
The little one stops to tie his shoe,
And they all go marching down to the ground
To get out of the rain, **boom, boom, boom!**

The ants go marching three by three, hurrah, hurrah!
The ants go marching three by three, hurrah, hurrah!
The ants go marching three by three,
The little one stops to climb a tree,
And they all go marching down to the ground
To get out of the rain, **boom, boom, boom!**

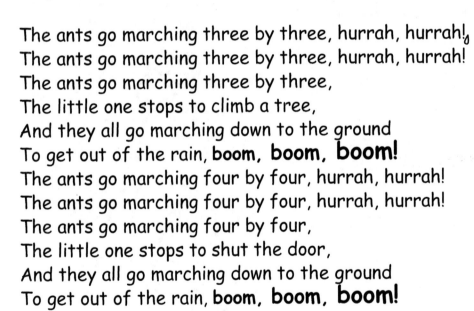

The ants go marching four by four, hurrah, hurrah!
The ants go marching four by four, hurrah, hurrah!
The ants go marching four by four,
The little one stops to shut the door,
And they all go marching down to the ground
To get out of the rain, **boom, boom, boom!**

The ants go marching five by five, hurrah, hurrah!
The ants go marching five by five, hurrah, hurrah!
The ants go marching five by five,
The little one stops to jump alive,
And they all go marching down to the ground
To get out of the rain, **boom, boom, boom!**

The Ants Go Marching *(cont.)*

The ants go marching six by six, hurrah, hurrah!
The ants go marching six by six, hurrah, hurrah!
The ants go marching six by six,
The little one stops to pick up sticks,
And they all go marching down to the ground
To get out of the rain, **boom, boom, boom!**

The ants go marching seven by seven, hurrah, hurrah!
The ants go marching seven by seven, hurrah, hurrah!
The ants go marching seven by seven,
The little one stops to look up to heaven,
And they all go marching down to the ground
To get out of the rain, **boom, boom, boom!**

The ants go marching eight by eight, hurrah, hurrah!
The ants go marching eight by eight, hurrah, hurrah!
The ants go marching eight by eight,
The little one stops to shut the gate,
And they all go marching down to the ground
To get out of the rain, **boom, boom, boom!**

The ants go marching nine by nine, hurrah, hurrah!
The ants go marching nine by nine, hurrah, hurrah!
The ants go marching nine by nine,
The little one stops to check the time,
And they all go marching down to the ground
To get out of the rain, **boom, boom, boom!**

The ants go marching ten by ten, hurrah, hurrah
The ants go marching ten by ten, hurrah, hurrah
The ants go marching ten by ten,
The little one stops to say "the end,"
And they all go marching down to the ground
To get out of the rain, **boom, boom, boom**

Suggested Instruments: Drums and Sticks

     #2002 *Music for Everyone*

Transition Songs

Transition songs help students move enthusiastically between activities. Some are geared for a specific activity, while others are more generic. Teach the children these songs and use one of them every time you are going to a new activity. Rather than have your musicians grab instruments, you might suggest clapping hands, snapping fingers, or some other action that can be done while moving to another activity.

Use these songs without instruments to help students prepare for recess, cleaning up, etc. Singing the songs can help students focus on their task and get everyone doing the same thing.

Group Time
(Sing to the tune of "London Bridge".)

Time for group time, let's sit down,
Let's sit down,
Let's sit down.
Time for group time, let's sit down,
And get ready.

We are ready to have fun,
To have fun,
To have fun.
We are ready to have fun,
Let's start learning!

Out to Recess
(Sing to the tune of "London Bridge.")

Out to recess we will go,
We will go,
We will go.
Out to recess we will go,
Walking calmly.

We will have a lot of fun,
Lot of fun,
Lot of fun.
We will have a lot of fun,
With all our friends.

Snack Time

(Sing to the tune of "London Bridge.")

Let's all wash our hands and sit

Snack time's here,

Time to eat.

We'll be clean and neat and say

Please and thank you.

Then we'll eat and talk with friends.

And clean up

At the end.

Crumbs and germs we'll wash away

After snack time.

Rest Time

(Sing to the tune of "Hot Cross Buns.")

Time to rest!

Time to rest!

Find a nice spot

And lie right down.

Time to rest!

Art Time

(Sing to the tune of "London Bridge.")

Time to create something new
Something new,
Something new.
Time to create something new
Let's get going.
Let's see what we'll make today
Make today,
Make today.
Let's see what we'll make today
Let's get busy!

Clean Up

(Sing to the tune of "London Bridge.")

It is time to clean the room,
Clean the room,
Clean the room,
It is time to clean the room,
Let's start cleaning!
Clean up all the mess we made,
Mess we made,
Mess we made,
Clean up all the mess we made,
Let's all clean up!

28

Line Up

(Sing to the tune of "London Bridge.")

Let's all line up at the door,

At the door,

At the door.

Let's all line up at the door,

It's time to go home.

Say goodbye to all our friends,

All our friends,

All our friends.

Say goodbye to all our friends

And our teacher.

Everyday Songs

Singing songs should be fun—an uplift during the day. The following songs are about everyday things that you can discuss in the classroom. They might go along with a unit of study or just be a song to sing for fun. All of the songs on the following pages use the tunes from "I'm a Little Teapot" or "Twinkle, Twinkle, Little Star."

Hello, Hello, Glad You're Here

(Sing and clap to the tune of "Twinkle, Twinkle, Little Star.")

Hello, hello, glad you're here.

Let's all give a little cheer.

We'll start singing lots of songs,

Having fun so come along.

Hello, hello, glad you're here.

Let's all give a little cheer!

30

ABC's and 123's

(Sing to the tune of "Twinkle, Twinkle, Little Star.")

ABC's and 123's,

Songs that make us slap our knees.

Books and games for everyone,

All join in to have some fun.

Crafts and painting are for me,

Come into our class and see.

School Has Started

(Sing to the tune of "Twinkle, Twinkle, Little Star.")

School has started again today,

Let's all cheer—Hooray! Hooray!

We'll make crafts and have a snack,

So much to do before we pack.

Let's get going and have some fun,

Our own school is number one!

Suggestion: Change the words "our own school" to the name of your school.
Example: "Meadowcreek is number one."

The Playground

(Sing to the tune of "I'm a Little Teapot.")

Out on the playground
I will go.
Walk until we get there
That I know.
I'll swing real high
And run around.
And spin in circles
Till I fall down.

Going to the Zoo

(Sing to the tune of "I'm a Little Teapot.")

I'm going to the zoo, I cannot wait.
The animals there
Are really great.
I want to see zebras,
Hear the lions roar,
See monkeys, seals, and so much more!

Dancing and Movement

Moving while singing songs is a lot of fun and a great way to get the wiggles out! The songs in this section have suggested movements listed in parentheses under the words. Use these simple movements (or change or add your own) to help your musicians really get into the songs.

She Sailed Away

(Traditional)

She sailed away on a bright and sunny day
On the back of a crocodile.
(Put hands together with thumbs pointing to the side, like a crocodile's mouth.)

"You see," said she, "He's as tame as he can be.
(Pet back of one hand with other hand.)

I'll ride him down the Nile."
(Move hands from side to side, like a crocodile moving through the water.)

The croc winked his eye
(Wink)

As he bade them all goodbye,
(Wave)

Wearing a happy smile.
(Pretend to draw a smile on your face,)

At the end of the ride,
(Move hands again.)

The lady was inside,
(Pat tummy.)

And the smile on the crocodile!
(Outline a smile on face again.)

Do Your Ears Hang Low?

Do Your Ears Hang Low?
(Traditional)

Do your ears hang low, do they wobble to and fro?
(Put hands on sides of face and move back and forth, like big floppy ears.)

Can you tie them in a knot, can you tie them in a bow?
(Pretend to tie a knot and bow in the air in front of you.)

Can you throw them over your shoulder, like a
continental soldier?
(Throw hands over a shoulder, then salute like a soldier.)

Do your ears hang low?
(Put hands at sides of face again.)

34

You Are My Sunshine

(Traditional)

You are my sunshine,
(Touch hands over your head.)

My only sunshine.
(Use arms to make a big circle overhead.)

You make me happy,
(Draw a smile on your face.)

When skies are gray.
(Move hands over head for sky.)

You'll never know, dear
(Shake head, no.)

How much I love you.
(Do sign language for "I love you.")

Please don't take
(Shake head, "no.")

My sunshine away!
(Make a circle with arms over head again.)

Sign Language: **I LOVE YOU!**

1. *Little finger on right hand sticking up for "I."*

2. *Make fists and cross them on your chest for "love".*

3. *Point with your index finger for "you."*

Head, Shoulders, Knees and Toes

Before singing "Heads, Shoulders, Knees and Toes," review the body parts mentioned in this song. Have students touch their heads, shoulders, knees, toes, eyes, ears, mouth, and nose. Then sing the song.

Head, Shoulders, Knees, and Toes

(Traditional)

Head, shoulders,

knees and toes, knees and toes.

Head, shoulders,

knees and toes, knees and toes.

Eyes and ears and mouth and nose.

Head, shoulders,

knees and toes, knees and toes.

Variations

- After the children know the song, you can have them try this version of the song. When they sing the song the first time, they say all the words and point to each body part. The second time singing the song they point to their heads, but don't say the word *head*. The second time through don't sing *head* or *shoulders*, but continue to touch heads and shoulders. The third time through don't sing *head*, *shoulders* or *knees*. The last time singing they don't sing *heads*, *shoulders*, *knees*, or *toes*.

- Another option with this action song is to sing the song several times in a row and get faster and faster each time. This is a fun way to burn some energy on those too-cold-to-play-outside kind of days!

36

My Hat, It Has Three Corners

(Traditional)

My hat, it has three corners,
Three corners has my hat.
And had it not three corners,
It would not be my hat.

Motions

Touch your head when you sing the word *hat*.
For three, hold up three fingers.
Touch your elbows for the word *corners*.

Directions

1. Fold a piece of construction paper in half. Place the pattern on the folded edge of the construction paper. Trace the pattern. Copy the pattern three times for each tri-corner hat being made.
2. Lay the three patterns flat and smooth out the creases.
3. Staple the patterns end-to-end, creating a triangle shape. Adjust to fit.
4. Add decorations.

Tri-Corner Hat Pattern

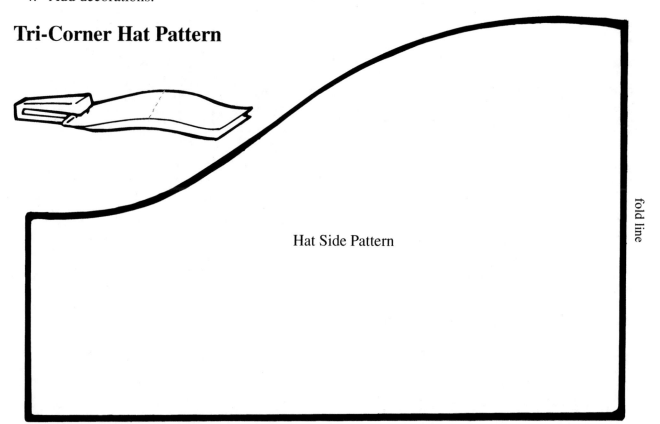

Hat Side Pattern

fold line

Where Is Thumbkin?

(Traditional)

Where is Thumbkin, where is Thumbkin?
(Hold hands behind back.)

Here I am, here I am!
(Bring one hand from behind your back with the thumb pointing up, then bring the other one out.)

"How are you today, sir?"
(Thumbs facing each other, move one thumb at a time, so it looks like the thumbs are talking to each other.)

"Very well, I thank you,"
(Thumbs facing each other, move so it looks like they are talking to each other again.)

Run away, run away!
(Hide one hand behind back and then the other.)

Extension

Continue singing the song using the following names for the rest of the fingers. Use the featured finger to carry out the actions.

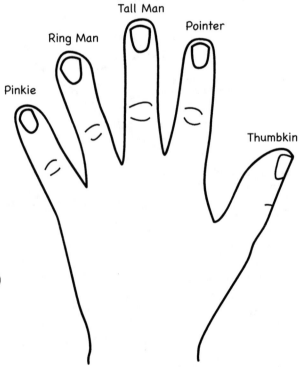

Where is Pointer? *(index finger)*
Where is Tall Man? *(middle finger)*
Where is Ring Man? *(ring finger)*
Where is Pinkie? *(pinkie finger)*

Hokey Pokey

(Traditional)

You put your right hand in,

You put your right hand out,

You put your right hand in,

And you shake it all about.

You do the Hokey Pokey,

And you turn yourself around.

That's what it's all about!

Variations

Listed below are the other body parts that can be substituted for "right hand," or be creative and come up with some of your own. This song is a great one for moving about, reviewing body parts and directionality.

—left hand   —head

—right foot   —whole self

—left foot   —knee

—right hip   —elbow

Student Input Songs

The following songs allow the students to contribute to the song lyrics. In these songs, the children get to choose the words they are singing or the actions or sound effects involved. Adding new rhymes to existing songs is a great way to work on rhyming too!

How Much Is that Doggie in the Window?

(Traditional)

How much is that doggie in the window?
The one with the waggly tail.
How much is that doggie in the window?
I do hope that doggie's for sale.

Variation

Teach the students this song. Then let your musicians decide what animal is in the window and what sound that animal makes. For example: How much is that kitty in the window—*meow meow*. You can also let them choose the characteristic of the animal they are singing about. Instead of a wagging tail, it could be big teeth for a lion, funny feet for a duck, etc.

The end result could be:

How much is that kitty in the window?
— meow meow
The one with the pretty long tail.
How much is that kitty in the window?
—meow meow
I do hope that kitty's for sale.

She'll Be Coming 'Round the Mountain

(Traditional)

She'll be coming 'round the mountain when she comes, **"Yee haw!"**
She'll be coming 'round the mountain when she comes, **"Yee haw!"**
She'll be coming 'round the mountain,
She'll be coming 'round the mountain,
She'll be coming 'round the mountain when she comes, **"Yee haw!"**

She'll be driving six white horses when she comes, **"Whoa back!"**
She'll be driving six white horses when she comes, **"Whoa back!"**
She'll be driving six white horses,
She'll be driving six white horses,
She'll be driving six white horses when she comes,
"Whoa back!" "Yee Haw!"

Oh, we'll all go out and meet her when she comes, **"Hi, Babe!"**
Oh, we'll all go out and meet her when she comes, **"Hi, Babe!"**
Oh, we'll all go out and meet her,
Oh, we'll all go out and meet her,
Oh, we'll all go out and meet her when she comes,
"Hi, Babe!" "Whoa back!" "Yee Haw!"

We'll all have chicken and dumplings when she comes, **"Yum, Yum"**
We'll all have chicken and dumplings when she comes, **"Yum, Yum"**
We'll all have chicken and dumplings,
We'll all have chicken and dumplings
We'll all have chicken and dumplings when she comes,
"Yum, Yum!" "Hi Babe!" "Whoa back!" Yee Haw!"

Variations

Teach the song to your musicians. Let them give suggestions to create a new version.

- They can choose what she'll be driving. It could be cars, riding an animal, etc. For example: She'll be driving six fast race cars when she comes—*vroom, vroom,* or she'll be riding on a monkey when she comes—*eee, eee.*

- They can also choose what she will be eating instead of chicken and dumplings. For example: We'll all have lots of hot dogs when she comes—*yum yum.*

The Bear in the Forest

(Sing to the tune of "The Wheels on the Bus.")

The bear in the forest says *grr grr grr,*
  grr grr grr,
  grr grr grr.
The bear in the forest says *grr grr grr,*
All through the day.

The bird in the forest says *chirp chirp chirp,*
  chirp chirp chirp,
  chirp chirp chirp.
The bird in the forest says *chirp chirp chirp,*
All through the day.

The monkey in the zoo says *eee eee eee,*
  eee eee eee,
  eee eee eee.
The monkey in the zoo says *eee eee eee,*
All through the day.

Variations

For an interesting twist, you can also sing about things in a house.

  For example:

  The broom in the house goes *sweep sweep sweep...*

  The sink in the house goes *drip drip drip...*

  The mom in the house says *go to sleep...*

  The chair in the house goes *squeak squeak squeak...*

    42

If You're Happy and You Know It

(Traditional)

If you're happy and you know it,
    clap your hands! *(clap, clap)*
If you're happy and you know it,
    clap your hands! *(clap, clap)*
If you're happy and you know it, then your face will surely show it.
(Smile and poke fingers at cheeks to make dimples.)
If you're happy and you know it,
    clap your hands! *(clap, clap)*

If you're sad and you know it,
    cry boo hoo. *("Boo hoo")*
If you're sad and you know it,
    cry boo hoo. *("Boo hoo")*
If you're sad and you know it, then your face will surely show it.
(Wipe eyes like you are crying.)
If you're sad and you know it,
    cry boo hoo. *("Boo hoo")*

If you're excited and you know it,
    shout hooray! *("Hooray!")*
If you're excited and you know it,
    shout hooray! *("Hooray!")*
If you're excited and you know it, then your face will surely show it.
If you're excited and you know it,
    shout hooray! *("Hooray!")*

If you're mad and you know it,
    stomp your feet! *(stomp, stomp)*
If you're mad and you know it,
    stomp your feet! *(stomp, stomp)*
If you're mad and you know it, then your face will surely show it.
If you're mad and you know it,
    stomp your feet! *(stomp, stomp)*

Old McDonald

(Traditional)

Old McDonald had a farm, *e-i, e-i, o.*
And on his farm he had a cow, *e-i, e-i, o.*
With a *moo moo* here,
And a *moo moo* there.
Here a *moo,* there a *moo,*
Everywhere a *moo, moo.*
Old McDonald had a farm, *e-i, e-i, o.*

Old McDonald had a farm, *e-i, e-i, o.*
And on his farm he had a pig, *e-i, e-i, o.*
With an *oink, oink* here,
And an *oink, oink* there.
Here an *oink,* there an *oink,*
Everywhere an *oink, oink.*
Old McDonald had a farm, *e-i, e-i, o.*

Old McDonald had a farm, *e-i, e-i, o.*
And on his farm he had a hen, *e-i, e-i, o.*
With a *cluck, cluck* here,
And a *cluck, cluck* there.
Here a *cluck,* there a *cluck,*
Everywhere a *cluck, cluck.*
Old McDonald had a farm, *e-i, e-i, o.*

Variations
- Give students the opportunity to choose what kinds of animals they are going to be on the farm. Discuss what sounds each animal makes.
- Change the venue. What animals might Old McDonald have in a zoo, or a rainforest?

Songs for Seasons

Fall or autumn suggests falling leaves. Encourage your musicians to move and sway like falling leaves while singing.

Fall Time is Here

(Sing two rounds to the tune of "Ring Around the Rosie.")

Ring around the leaf pile, pocketful of leaves.

Jumping, jumping, we all fall down!

The trees are in the meadow, shedding colorful leaves,

Raking, raking, fall time is here!

Leaves

(Sing to the tune of "I'm a Little Teapot.")

In fall I love to watch the leaves,

As they fall down from the trees.

I'll rake them all up really fast,

So I can jump in and have a blast!

Songs for Seasons *(cont.)*

Winter Fun

(Sing to the tune of "I'm a Little Teapot.")

Snowflakes are falling,
Down they go.
It's fun to be outside
In the snow.
I'm glad I have a coat and mittens too,
But I have some cold snow in my shoe.

I'll make a snowman,
Watch me roll.
I'll give him two eyes
Made out of coal.
A carrot for his nose and then a hat,
Now what do you really think of that?

I have a snowman
Short and fat.
Here are his buttons
Here is his hat.
When I go outside, he plays with me,
When I go inside, he goes to sleep!

Suggestion: The three verses can be sung as a three-verse song, or you may wish to sing them separately.

Songs for Seasons *(cont.)*

Spring is all about growing and spreading out. See what actions your musicians will come up with for these songs.

Mow, Mow, Mow the Lawn

(Sing to the tune of "Row, Row, Row Your Boat.")

Mow, mow, mow the lawn,

Smell the flowers too.

New life abounds on the earth

In spring for me and you.

The Flower Song

(Sing to the tune of "Twinkle Twinkle, Little Star.")

Flowers start to grow and grow

Breezes move them to and fro.

They will grow up to the sky.

Watch them grow as time goes by.

Purple, yellow, white and red

Colors in the flower bed.

Songs for Seasons *(cont.)*

Summer Fun
(Sing to the tune of "I'm a Little Teapot.")

Summer's almost here—games and fun.

I'll play all day out in the sun.

I can ride my bike and swing outside,

And slide down fast on a giant slide.

Summer's Here at Last
(Sing to the tune of "Ring Around the Rosies.")

Ring around the castles,
Pocket full of sand,
Dig holes, make roads,
We all lend a hand!
Water is salty,
And cool to the touch,
Splashes, splashes,
We love summer so much!

Holiday Songs

The Pumpkin

(Sing to the tune of "I'm a Little Teapot.")

Here's a special pumpkin,

Big and round.

He sits so heavy

On the hard ground.

I want to carve him,

Yes I do,

So then he will smile

And so will you!

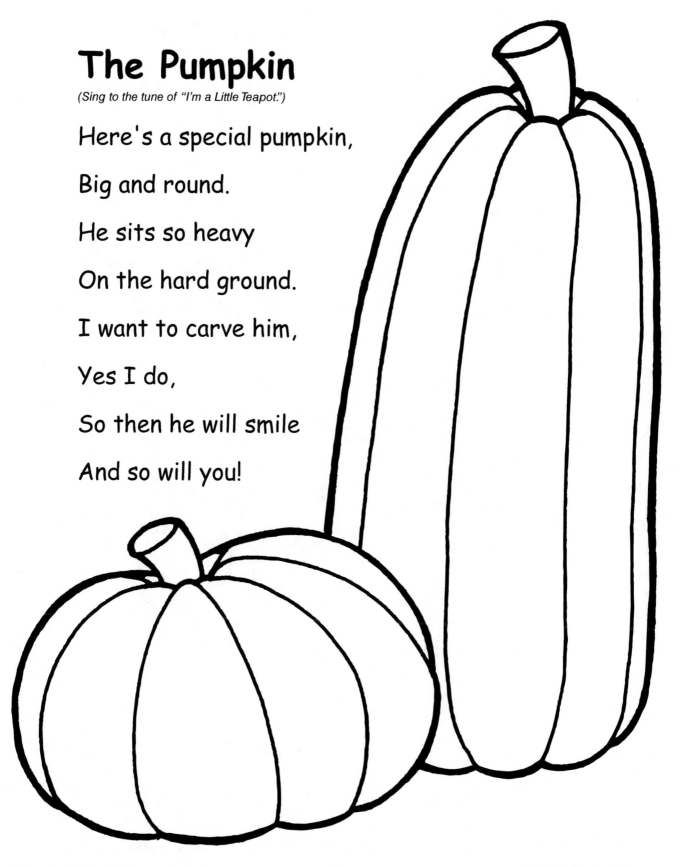

Holiday Songs *(cont.)*

The Turkey

(Sing to the tune of "I'm a Little Teapot.")

I have a turkey

Big and fat.

He spreads his wings

And he walks like that.

His daily corn he will not miss,

And when he walks he talks like this—

"Gobble, gobble, gobble."

50

Holiday Songs *(cont.)*

Holiday Time is Near
(Sing to the tune of "Row, Row, Row Your Boat.")

Holiday time is near,

Let's all give a cheer!

Family, family, family, family,

When are they getting here?

Holiday Songs (cont.)

Valentine's Day

(Sing to the tune of "I'm a Little Teapot.")

It's Valentine's Day,

So much fun.

Cards for parents,

Daughters and sons.

I'll send some to friends, you will see

What fun Valentine's Day will be!

Holiday Songs *(cont.)*

Easter Is Coming

(Sing to the tune of "Christmas is Coming.")

Easter is coming,

It's time for spring and more.

Time to put the decorations on the door.

It's time to color Easter eggs

And hide them all around

I hope the Easter bunny comes

And hops upon the ground!

The Green Grass Grew All Around

(Traditional)

Preparation

Create a tree in your classroom to serve as a guide when learning this performance song. Using the patterns provided on pages 58–64, create a hole, roots, a tree, a separate branch with twigs, a nest, an egg and a bird. Add green grass around the base of the tree. When singing the song, give different students an opportunity to point to the different items mentioned in the song. Later, students may make separate patterns to hold up for the different verses.

Presentation

Before introducing this song, ask the children if they know what an echo is. Explain that an echo is a repetition. Teach the children that this song is an echo song. Every time the teacher sings a part of the song, the students will "echo" the same words.

For example, when the teacher sings, "There was a hole" the students will repeat the words, singing, "There was a hole" in the same melody. The only part of the song that isn't echoed is, "Well the _____ is in the _____, and the refrain.

This song builds upon itself. Each time a new verse is sung, the other verses are repeated. Musicians will have to remember what they sang in the verse before, so they can add to it the next time.

When singing this song, the teacher may choose to sing the words and the echo of the words. Add the arm and hand motions suggested for each line once students are comfortable with the lyrics. Props can also be used.

Suggested hand motions for specific lines:

There was a hole.—*Connect hands in front of you to create a circle.*

That you ever did see.—*Make binoculars with your hands.*

And the green grass grew all around.—*Ripple hands in front of you to symbolize the grass.*

Verses

There was a root—*Wiggle fingers.*

There was a tree—*Raise hands above head to look like a tree with branches.*

There was a branch—*Hold up one arm for a branch.*

There was a nest—*Cup hands together to form a bowl.*

There was an egg—*Clasp hands tightly together to form a ball.*

There was a bird—*Flap arms like wings.*

The Green Grass Grew All Around

(Traditional)

There was a hole *(echo)*
In the middle of the ground *(echo)*
The prettiest hole *(echo)*
That you ever did see *(echo)*

Refrain

And the green grass grew all around, all around,
And the green grass grew all around.

Now in this hole *(echo)*
There was a root *(echo)*
The prettiest root *(echo)*
That you ever did see *(echo)*
Well, the root's in the hole,
And the hole's in the ground,

Refrain

And the green grass grew all around, all around,
And the green grass grew all around.

Now on this root *(echo)*
There was a tree *(echo)*
The prettiest tree *(echo)*
That you ever did see *(echo)*

Well, the tree's on the root,
And the root's in the hole,
And the hole's in the ground,

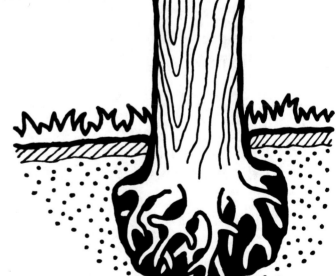

Refrain

And the green grass grew all around, all around,
And the green grass grew all around.

The Green Grass Grew All Around (cont.)

Now on this tree *(echo)*
There was a branch *(echo)*
The prettiest branch *(echo)*
That you ever did see *(echo)*

Well, the branch is on the tree,
And the tree's on the root,
And the root's in the hole,
And the hole's in the ground,

Refrain

And the green grass grew all around, all around,
And the green grass grew all around.

Now on this branch *(echo)*
There was a nest *(echo)*
The prettiest nest *(echo)*
That you ever did see *(echo)*

Well, the nest's on the branch,
And the branch is on the tree,
And the tree's on the root,
And the root's in the hole,
And the hole's in the ground,

Refrain

And the green grass grew all around, all around,
And the green grass grew all around.

56

The Green Grass Grew All Around *(cont.)*

Now in this nest *(echo)*
There was an egg *(echo)*
The prettiest egg *(echo)*
That you ever did see *(echo)*

Well, the egg's in the nest,
And the nest's on the branch,
And the branch is on the tree,
And the tree's on the root,
and the root's in the hole,
And the hole's in the ground,

Refrain

And the green grass grew all around, all around,
And the green grass grew all around.

Now in this egg *(echo)*
There was a bird *(echo)*
The prettiest bird *(echo)*
That you ever did see *(echo)*

Well, the bird's in the egg,
And the egg's in the nest,
And the nest's on the branch,
And the branch is on the tree,
And the tree's on the root,
And the root's in the hole,
And the hole's in the ground,

Refrain

And the green grass grew all around, all around,
And the green grass grew all around.

Hole

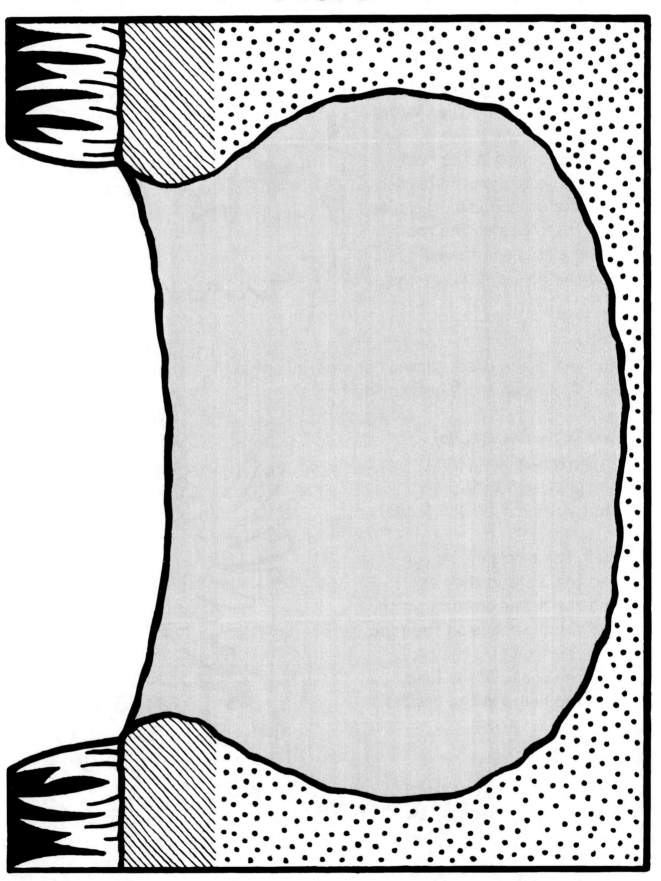

Roots

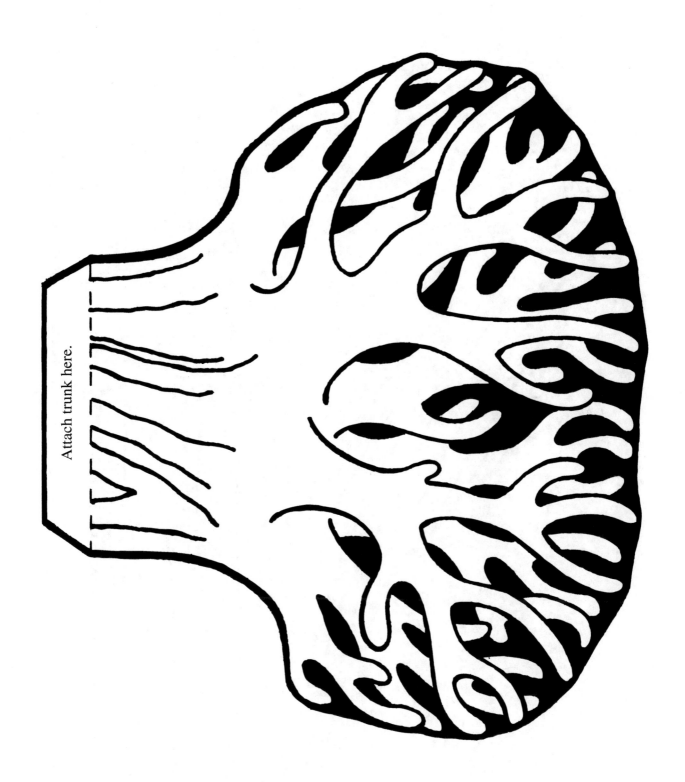

Attach trunk here.

Tree

Attach branch here.

Branch

Nest

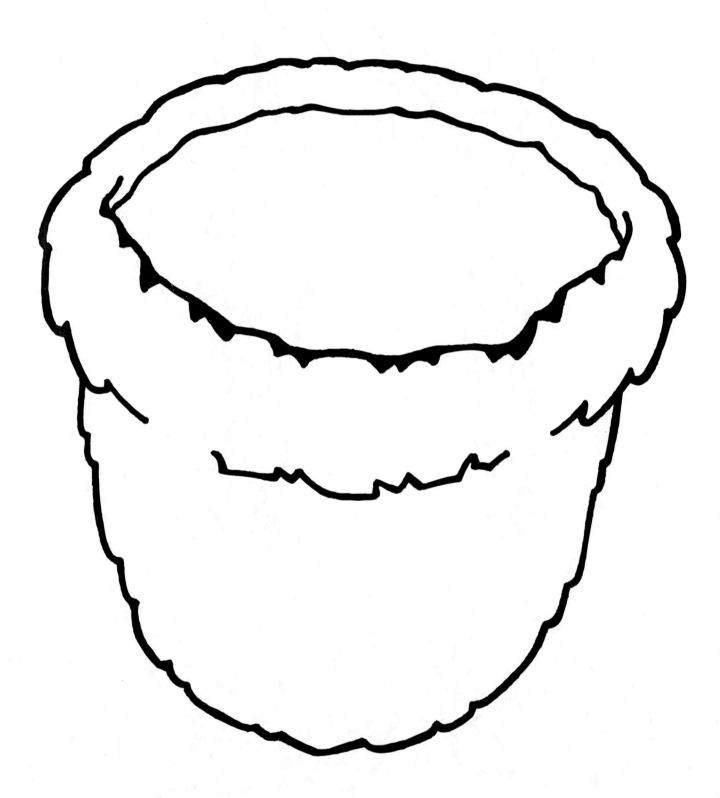

Egg

Bird

64